My Mother

*So much of what I have become
is because of you
and I want you to know
that I appreciate you, thank you
and love you
more than words can express*

— Susan Polis Schutz

SPS Studios, Inc.

P.O. Box 4549, Boulder, Colorado 80306

A Mother's Love Is Forever

Featuring poems by
Susan Polis Schutz
and Donna Fargo

Blue Mountain Press™

SPS Studios, Inc., Boulder, Colorado

To the Best Mother of All...
My Mom

*I*f I had to pick one thing
about you, Mom,
that makes you so special,
I don't think it would be possible.
I couldn't begin to count
the number of times
you tolerated my moods,
consoled my heartbreaks
and disappointments,
endured my ups and downs,
listened to words confused by tears,
and just simply understood
for no other reason
than because you love me.
The years hold precious memories,
but most of all, they hold growth.
In a way, we grew up together.
There's still some growing left to do,
but one thing becomes more clear to me
with each passing day,
and I hope you know:
there's no other mom like you,
and I love you very much.

— Susan M. Pavlis

I Wish I Could
Do This for You, Mom

I wish I could make sure
   you always had the best —
like laughter, rainbows,
   butterflies, and health.
I wish I could take you anywhere
   you wanted to go
and treat you to waterfalls,
   rivers, forests, and mountaintops.
I wish I could make it possible for you
to do anything you ever dreamed of,
   even if just for a day.
I wish I could keep you from
   ever being hurt or sad,
and that all your troubles
   and problems would disappear.

I wish that I could package up
all the memories that bring smiles to you
and have them handy for
      your immediate enjoyment.
I wish I could guarantee you peace of mind,
      contentment, faith, and strength,
as well as the constant ability
      to find joy in all the things
that sometimes go unnoticed.
I wish you moments to connect
      with other individuals
who are full of smiles and hugs to give away
and stories and laughter to share.
I wish you could always know
      how much you mean to me —
because no matter what's going on in our lives,
you are loved and appreciated.

— Barbara Cage

Thank You, Mother

I've been much too busy with other things in my life lately. I have taken your love for granted. Haven't been considerate enough. Haven't said "Thank you" enough. But I hope you will receive these words from me now...

Thank you for the sacrifices you have made for me. Thank you for all you've given me and all you've done for me.

I know there have been times that, had it not been for your unselfishness, my life would have been different: not as balanced, not as happy.

Thank you for giving me life. Thank you for your example. Thank you for being my mother. I wouldn't trade you even if I could. I love you so much.

— Donna Fargo

To My Mother

When you have a mother
who cares so much for you
that anything you want
comes before her desires
When you have a mother
who is so understanding that
no matter what is bothering you
she can make you smile
When you have a mother
who is so strong that
no matter what obstacles she faces
she is always confident in front of you
When you have a mother
who actively pursues her goals in life
but includes you in all her goals
you are very lucky indeed
Having a mother like this
makes it easy to grow up
into a loving, strong adult
Thank you for
being this kind
of wonderful
mother

— Susan Polis Schutz

In You, Mom,
I've Seen Everything
that Love Can Be

I've seen tears in your eyes — tears for my suffering, my happiness, and my disappointments. I've seen hope on your face — hope for my wishes, my blessings, and my best.

I've seen anger on your face, too — when you felt that someone was treating me unfairly, or when I was using bad judgment and you knew that I was hurting myself. I've seen joy in your eyes — when I reached for the stars and caught the moon, stars and all!

I've seen enthusiasm in you — when I was feeling inspired, self-assured, and certain that I could do anything that I set out to do.

I've seen disappointment in you — when
I tried but didn't achieve the thing I had set
out to do, or when I lost something special
to me and there was no way to help.

I've seen determination in you — when
you wanted to be sure that I was happy.
Whatever it might have cost you, I believe
that you would have offered it gladly if you
had to sacrifice it for my happiness.

I've seen strength in you — when I
needed you to help me. I've felt the joy of
your acceptance and understanding. I've
known the warmth and comfort of having
you there — always willing to give whatever
I needed from you.

I've seen so much love in you — a love
that is unconditional. Thank you, Mom.
I love you, too.

— Regina Hill

To an Amazing Mother

You're so thoughtful and kind and loving, such a wonderful example. I'm lucky to have you for a mother.

I want you to always be safe and happy and content and healthy. I want you to know how great I think you are. I know your life hasn't always been easy, but I appreciate the way you raised me. Nothing compares to the unselfish love you've shown.

If I could, I'd make your every dream come true today and grant every secret wish you have. I'd like to surprise you with your heart's desire just so I could see you grin from ear to ear, cry tears of joy, and feel the depth of my love.

Words could never express how thankful I am that you're my mother and how very much I love you. I hope you have a very special day doing whatever you want to do and feeling loved through and through.

— Donna Fargo

You Are Everything
a Mother Should Be

A mother should be
strong and guiding
understanding and giving
A mother should be
honest and forthright
confident and able
A mother should be
relaxed and soft
flexible and tolerant
But most of all
a mother should be a
loving woman
who is always there when needed
Mom, you are a rare
and wonderful woman
You are everything
that a mother should be
and more

— Susan Polis Schutz

Your Love Will
Live Forever Within Me

You gave me life, nurtured and cared for me, and when you felt the time was right, you set me free. Through the years, never once did you complain or wish for things to be any different. You simply took your life in stride, no questions asked, embracing the happy moments along with the sad, accepting all things for what they were. That was your way.

I didn't always understand or appreciate everything you did. I was a child with my own innocent perception of the world. Now, as a grownup, I can reflect with such admiration and respect on the wonderful woman and mother you were then and still are today.

You stood with courage to meet the responsibilities that fell upon you, and sacrificed so much for the love of your children. What you have accomplished is more than you will ever realize. When I think of all that you have done for our family and all the love you have so generously poured from your heart, I feel humbled. There will never be enough gratitude to offer to you or a means to repay you. But my heart will always be filled with the joy of knowing your love. It is the most precious gift I have ever received, for it is the one you have so wisely taught me to set free and share with others.

I love you for being a caring person, a remarkable woman, and an exceptional mother. This love that you have given will forever live within me. Thank you for being my mother.

— debbie peddle

What Is a Mother's Love?

A mother's love is many things. She is a teacher and a friend, someone to guide you through right and wrong, someone to listen and understand.

She can comfort you like no other, holding you in her arms. She can fill your spirit with confidence and encourage your unsure heart.

She can bring a smile to your saddened face, wipe away your tears, love you regardless of the faults you have, and stand by you throughout the years.

A mother's love is many things, and one thing is quite sure: a mother's love is special, for no one can love like her.

— T. L. Nash

It Takes Someone Special
— Just like You —
to Raise a Child

To raise a child to be a person of worth requires a parent's caring use of so many special talents...

It requires someone who understands that a child has feelings that change from day to day, and each feeling needs love and nurturing.

It requires someone to receive those feelings as they would their own — handling each with honesty, gentleness, and care.

It takes a heart above the rest of the world to see a child's potential, to draw it out, to encourage their dreams, and to help with their plans.

To raise a child to be a person of worth takes someone who makes it a point to be that child's caring confidant.

It takes someone exactly like YOU to give a child so many reasons to believe they're a special someone on this earth... and your child will always appreciate your efforts.

— Barbara J. Hall

I Hope I've Been
the Kind of Child You
Always Wanted

So many years have passed between us
    since the first time you held me
and told me you would always love me.
So many memories have brought us
    close together over the years.
There was a time in my life when you
pulled me as close as you could
    to your heart,
because you felt I needed you.
Thank you — I did.
There were times in my life when
I needed your strength to walk
and your vision to see.
Thank you for being there for me.
However, your honesty is the most
valuable quality I have gained
    from you over the years.

It has helped me to see who I am,
and it helps me enable others
    to accept themselves. Thank you.
There are many other wonderful qualities
you have given to me through your love,
and I hope I have said "thank you"
    for them along the way.
Every day, I think about how fortunate
I am to have a mother as special as you
    in my life.
If I could ever choose to start my life
    over again,
I wouldn't change a thing
except the number of times I've told
    you "I love you" —
for that can't be expressed enough.
I hope that I have been the child
    you always wanted,
because you are the mother
I will always love.
                    — Antony Simpson

For You, Mom, Forever

You are my greatest inspiration.
You are my one-of-a-kind wonder.
You are someone who has touched my life
    with more caring than others could ever
    be capable of and more understanding
    than I will ever deserve.
You are an angel in my life.
You are a source of joy for my tomorrows.
You are a million memories from my past.
You are a positive influence on my days and
    on my dreams in a way that will always last.

You are the greatest gift I will ever know.
You're the place where love comes from.
I could tell you this every day and still not say
                how much...

                I love you, Mom.
                                    — K. D. Stevens

You are a remarkable woman
accomplishing so much as a
strong woman
in a man's world
strong but soft
strong but caring
strong but compassionate

You are a remarkable woman
accomplishing so much as a
giving woman
in a selfish world
giving to your friends
giving to your family
giving to everyone

You are a remarkable woman
who is also a remarkable mother
who is loved by so many people
whose lives you have touched
including mine

— Susan Polis Schutz

A Special Thank-You

I know I'm not your responsibility anymore. I'm all grown up... on my own... responsible for myself now and accountable for the consequences of my own actions. But I want you to know that you'll always be with me, in every decision I make.

You are always in my thoughts, in my heart, and on my mind. I know that my life is easier now because you were so good to me. I am happier, more balanced, and less afraid.

I know I've told you before, but I want to thank you once again for being my mother, for treating me so well, and for believing in me.

Your love and approval shaped my destiny, nurtured me, and helped my dreams to take flight. I still lean on the lessons I learned in my childhood and the feeling that you thought I was special. I don't know what I'd have done without you, who I would be without your positive influence, or where I'd be now. I am so thankful for you.

I appreciated you then, and I appreciate you even more now. If I could, I'd give you the world, make all your dreams come true, and cause your life to be fulfilled in every place something is missing. I love you so much, and I just wanted you to hear it from me again: Thank you so much for being the best mother in the world.

— Donna Fargo

Because of You...

$\mathcal{I}$'ve known a mother's love.
   I've sensed a mother's warm concern,
and I've been on the receiving end
   of a mother's friendship.
Because of you, I've been
   influenced by someone
I look up to with deep respect
   and total admiration.
You've always let me know that you
   care for me in the greatest way,
because you've given me a mother's love.

Today, I'm letting you know something
   I hope you've always been aware of:
      You mean the world to me,
         and you always will.
      Thank you for offering me
         a mother's love.
      I love you very much.

— Barbara J. Hall

Mom, I'm working hard to build
the kind of life
you raised me to believe in;
I'm following some dreams
that have always mattered to me.
The more I do, the more I realize
    how much I'm using
what you taught me about the world.
You deserve a world of thanks
    for everything you've given to me:
courage to take chances (even to fail),
confidence to expect the best of myself,
and a profound sense of the joy that can
    be found in every day.
For all this and more,
I want to dedicate to you today
the greatest goal I could ever achieve
    in my life:
to make you proud of me.

— Edmund O'Neill

A mother has eyes in the
back of her head
and x-ray vision.
She always knows what is going on —
you can't fool her;
she can see right through your lies.

A mother has ears that hear
the smallest whimper at 2:00 a.m.,
crickets at dusk, and
the silent song of love.

A mother's hands are strong enough
to lift you up when you fall down,
but tender enough to bandage a scrape.

A mother may have narrow shoulders,
but they are broad enough to bear
your burdens as well as hers.

A mother's heart is easily broken,
but just as easily mended again
with two simple words: "I'm sorry."
Her well of love sometimes runs dry,
but is refilled daily by hugs and kisses.

Every mother is always "working";
she could use a day off,
    but rarely gets one
(and feels guilty when she does).

A mother's faith is blessed.
She'll never give up on you;
she'll keep you in her prayers
through good times and bad.

Having a mother and being a mother
are gifts from God.
There is no other job as frustrating
or as fulfilling.
                        — Linda H. Feinberg

From My Heart, Mother...

There are many things I wish I'd said to you as I was growing up and some things I wish I hadn't done. I know now that I missed many opportunities to say "Thank you," "I love you," and "What can I do?" There are many times I missed the mark in praising you for the good things that you've done. But knowing you, you didn't even notice, and I can only hope you'll hear what I'm trying to say now.

I love you, Mother. You gave me life, a chance to grow up and be whatever I could be. To me there's no one like you, and I'm so thankful you're <u>my</u> mother. You passed on to me your gentle spirit, your generosity, your passion for life, and your love. And I don't know of any greater gifts that anyone could receive.

So, Mother, I turn the tables now.
I give you back with all of me... my
generosity for being so unselfish with
your life. I thank you for every lesson
you have taught me about how to cope
with life and how not to. I thank you
for overlooking my faults and helping
me to move along in my own time. I
thank you for accepting me and treating
me so gently and fairly, but I thank you
most of all for your love. It is precious
to me, and indeed it is what life is all
about. I know I am so lucky. Yes, I thank
you for this heart you filled with love.

— Donna Fargo

Between a mother and child,
there is a special love
that exists nowhere else.
A mother is someone who loves
and is never afraid to show that love.
A mother sometimes pushes aside
    her own needs
to focus on the needs of others.
A mother is a haven of love,
    a listening ear when no one else cares
        or has time to listen.
A mother makes time.
A mother gives advice when asked
but always with the understanding
that it is only advice,
leaving her child free
to make his or her own choices.
Though there are some times
when mother and child don't agree,
a mother respects her child's choices,
encourages her child's decisions,
and listens to her child's reasoning.
A mother is all these things
to her child, and more.

— Dale Harcombe

Though We've Had Our Disagreements, I'll Always Love You, Mom

I know we haven't always
seen eye to eye, but that's okay.
Through all the happy moments
as well as the difficult ones,
I've always thought that you
were a good mother who wanted
what was best for me.
I know there have been times
when we had some problems communicating.
I haven't always agreed with everything
you said and did,
but I'm realizing now that
you're more than just my mother.
You are an individual,
unique in your own way —
a woman with your own feelings, hopes,
and dreams.

Now that I'm older, I'm beginning
to understand what you went through.
I may not need you in the same ways
I did when I was a child,
but I still need your support,
occasional advice, and always your love.
No matter what happens,
you'll always be my mother
and I'll always be your child —
and together, I want us to always be friends.

— Penny D. Kaplan

Thank You, Mom

I want to apologize
for any problems
that I may have caused you
in the past
I am not
the easiest person
to live with
since I am so
independent and strong
but you can be sure
that though it possibly
didn't seem like it
your values and ideals
did pass on to me
and I carry them forward
in all that I do

You always were someone
stable, strong, giving and warm
an ideal person to look up to
This has given me the
strength to lead
my own life
according to my own standards
Your leadership and love
have enabled me to grow
into a very
happy person
and I think that is
what every mother wishes
for her child
Thank you
      — Susan Polis Schutz

*W*herever we go,
and whatever we do,
let us live with this
remembrance in our hearts...
that we are family.

What we give to one another
comes full circle.
May we always be
the best of friends;
may we always be one another's
rainbow on a cloudy day;
as we have been yesterday
and today to each other,
may we be so blessed
in all our tomorrows...
over and over again...

For we are a family,
and that means love
that has no end.

— Collin McCarty

The love
of a family
is so
uplifting

The warmth
of a family
is so
comforting

The support
of a family
is so reassuring

The attitude
of a family
towards
each other
molds one's
attitude forever
towards the
world

— Susan Polis Schutz

A Mother Is...

A mother is life at its best. She understands. She goes a million miles out of her way just to lend a hand. She brings you smiles when a smile is exactly what you needed. She listens, and she hears what is said in the spaces between the words. A mother cares, and she lets you know you're in her prayers.

A mother can guide you, inspire you, comfort you, and light up your life. A mother understands your moods and nurtures your needs. She lovingly knows just what would help make things right.

A mother always knows the perfect thing to do.
She can make your whole day just by saying
something that no one else could have said.
Sometimes you feel like the two of you share a
secret language that others can't tune in to.

When your feelings come from deep inside and
need to be spoken to someone you don't have to
hide from, you share them with your mother.
When good news comes, she is the first one you
turn to. When feelings overflow and tears need
to fall, a mother helps you through it all.

A mother brings sunlight into your life. She
warms your life with her presence, whether she is
far away or close by your side. A mother is the
most wonderful gift that brings happiness, and a
treasure that money can't buy.

— Collin McCarty

Precious Mother, Sweetest Friend

When I'm about to give up, I think of you and I find the will to keep trying. When I feel unloved, I need only remember all you've done for me and I am touched again by your example. When I need a friend, I know there's someone who loves me and will accept me with loving arms no matter what I've done or haven't done.

Your life is a testament to love. I know now that there were times when you sacrificed your time, your energy, and maybe even your dreams just so you could give to me, and your unselfishness still amazes me. Even when I wasn't sensitive to your own needs and I acted less than perfect, you always gave so much. The example of your life reveals the most loving heart and the sweetest kind of friendship, unlike any other I've ever known.

If these feelings could paint a picture, everyone could see that I have the most precious mother in all the world and the sweetest friend.

— Donna Fargo

I Love You Forever, Mom

You have shown me how to give of myself
  You have shown me leadership
You have taught me to be strong
You have taught me the importance of the family
You have demonstrated unconditional love
You have demonstrated a sensitivity to people's needs
You have handed down to me the important
    values in life
You have handed down to me the idea of
    achieving one's goals
You have set an example, throughout your life
of what a mother and woman should be like
I am so proud of you
and I love you
forever

— Susan Polis Schutz

The Greatest Gift
You Have Ever Given Me...
Is Your Love

I've changed a lot throughout my life,
always learning a little more about myself
and the world around me.
The challenges were interesting
and sometimes overwhelming,
but I always believed in myself enough
to get me through the hard times.
One of the things
that I've come to know now,
after all those changes,
is that I never once doubted
whether you'd be there for me
if I needed you.
And there were many times
when I did need you,
and you were there.

When I was headstrong and defiant,
you watched me strive for my independence,
knowing life's lessons are best learned
through personal experience.
When I was self-centered,
you watched me discover on my own
a broader outlook on life.
I came to understand life on my own terms
and to appreciate you even more
for the examples you set
and the lifestyle you've lived.
Having your unconditional love in my life
has made me feel secure and loved,
and that is the greatest gift
any parent could ever give.

— Dena Dilaconi

My Perfect Mother

Your heart is big. Your love is pure. You want the best for me and care about everything I'm going through. You often put my needs above your own and overlook my mistakes. You love me without condition. Whatever I am and whatever I do is okay with you. You accept me... all of me. You're more than I could have ever hoped for in a mother. You're my perfect mother, and I'm so thankful for you.

You're always there: to hear my complaints,
to share my joy, to feel my pain, to listen
to my latest adventure, to advise me, to
cry with me and hope for me and laugh
with me, to forgive me when I do something
dumb. I've never heard a harsh word from
you that wasn't justified. I've never seen
selfishness from you... only a mother
who gives her love freely, happily, joyfully,
and perfectly.

If I looked the world over, I could never
find a mother more perfect than you.
If I could choose anyone at all for my
mom, I'd choose you. I'm so lucky that
God put me in your family and gave me
you for a mother. After all, I wouldn't
be me, without you. You're my perfect
mother, and I love you and appreciate
you more than I could ever express. I
hope and pray that you're happy and that
your every dream comes true. I pray for
your perfect health and unlimited joy.

— Donna Fargo

You Work So Hard and Do So Much

You work so hard and do so much. And I know that you wonder sometimes — if anyone really appreciates the efforts you make on all those uphill climbs. Day in and day out you make the world a better place to be. And the people who are lucky enough to be in your life are the ones who get to see...

You're a very wonderful person with a truly gifted touch. You go a million miles out of your way and you always do so much... to make sure that other lives are easier and filled with happiness. Your caring could never be taken for granted because the people you're close to are blessed... with someone who works at a job well done to bring smiles to the day.

You're a special person who deserves more thanks than this could ever say.

— Jenn Davids

Mom,
I Want You to Know...

As a child, I took for granted that my life and my heart were safe in your hands. From the moment I was born, you loved me from the depths of your soul, no matter what I said or did. I didn't understand that as a child. I simply trusted you, and that in itself was probably the biggest compliment I could have given to you.

Now, as an adult, I realize what it means to truly love someone. And it warms my heart to know that no matter how I decide to live my life, what I succeed in, or how many times I fail, there is still one person in this world who will love me no matter what.

I don't tell you often enough how much I love you, Mom, or how grateful I am to have the gift of your love.

— April Adams

My Mother

For as long as I can remember
she has been by my side
to give me support
to give me confidence
to give me help

For as long as I can remember
she has always been the person
    I looked up to
so strong
so sensitive
so pretty

For as long as I can remember
and still today
she is everything a mother should be

For as long as I can remember
she has always provided stability
    within our family
full of laughter
full of tears
full of love

So much of what I have become
is because of you
and I want you to know
that I appreciate you, thank you
and love you
more than words can express

— Susan Polis Schutz

ACKNOWLEDGMENTS

The following is a partial list of authors whom the publisher especially wishes to thank for permission to reprint their works.

PrimaDonna Entertainment Corp. for the following by Donna Fargo: "Thank You, Mother," "My Perfect Mother," "From My Heart, Mother...," "To an Amazing Mother," "A Special Thank-You," and "Precious Mother, Sweetest Friend." Copyright © 1996, 1998, 1999, 2001 by PrimaDonna Entertainment Corp. All rights reserved.

T. L. Nash for "What Is A Mother's Love?" Copyright © 2001 by T. L. Nash. All rights reserved.

Barbara J. Hall for "It Takes Someone Special — Just like You — to Raise a Child." Copyright © 2001 by Barbara J. Hall. All rights reserved.

Linda H. Feinberg for "A mother has eyes in the back of her head...." Copyright © 2001 by Linda H. Feinberg. All rights reserved.

A careful effort has been made to trace the ownership of poems used in this anthology in order to obtain permission to reprint copyrighted materials and give proper credit to the copyright owners. If any error or omission has occurred, it is completely inadvertent, and we would like to make corrections in future editions provided that written notification is made to the publisher:

SPS STUDIOS, INC., P.O. Box 4549, Boulder, Colorado 80306.